BANDAGES

To : Lori Goree

Thank you for always
being supportive of
my dream.

Michael R. King

BANDAGES

Michael R. King

To order additional copies of this book, contact:
Xlibris Corporation
1-888-795-4274
www.Xlibris.com
Orders@Xlibris.com
96426

To my Family~ Thank you for the Love that saved my Heart.

CONTENTS

It cannot rain all of the time

Romantic happenings & starlight nights
Come from standing within heroic fights . . .

The flame intense, new purity it brings
The years & dreams that find delicious things . . .

Another worldly Love out of luminous desires
Born of Heart, raised within wild fires . . .

Uncommon Valor, Legendary strength within
Would be the result & Love would always win . . .

If only all Love starved souls should somehow find
That it cannot rain all of the time.

I will do Anything

I will do Anything,
     If you just do not leave me ~
         To go and be so free.
     If you would stick around awhile
         & Hold me while I smile . . .

I will do Anything,
     For You, I will give my life ~
         If you let me stay your wife
     For Us, I would tie down my soul
         & Give you complete control . . .

I will do Anything,
     To make this last forever & ever ~
         For our Love never to sever
     To let Us be as one heart
         & Always know that we are not apart . . .

I will do Anything . . .

The Longest Kiss Goodbye

I saw it in your eyes the moment it happened
When the light shining upon our time started to dim
Escaping through the edges of an elemental kiss
Neither one of us knowing it might be the kiss goodbye

. . .

Now, it has come to this-
Finding a way to let go of what we know
Holding back the desires to touch, to clutch
Affections galore to be given freely, no more . . .

I want you to know that it will just be a show
Continuing on, as if our time is not gone
There is no way I cannot Love you each day
You know me—I will always dream away.

The Devils Arrow

The arrow pierced it's prey swift
Like your light, I thought it was a gift
How could I have known that you were lying?
Until that smirk on your face as you left me, crying . . .

Your sour bitterness abandoned me, high & dry
The torment was so intense, I really should have died
You obliterated this Love that I so desperately needed
Are you happy now that you have completely succeeded?

Now, these affections are waiting in time to be freed
Thanks to your ever so careless, Seductifying deed
You have no soul, just a hollow, empty shell
It truly satisfies your lust to pull others into your Hell . . .

Too bad, I am not the push-over, let go person~
That You thought
So sad, when you pull that last petal~
He will Love You not.

~ Adrift ~

Ravenous for the lightning from your touch~

Let alone, other propensities & such~

I heard you laughing & I wondered . . .
   (ringing in my ears like thunder)

When was the last time I made you laugh?

It was as good as it could ever get
      From that first moment on the day we met . . .

                  I held it in my hand for a second
Thought I had a good grip~
      Letting it slip, it fell through my fingers . . .

(Damn how the loss of Love lingers).

GONE

Ice cold, Stone faced
            Emotions misplaced
My heart beats strong
            All day long . . .

As I let go the need to know
            My fantasy begins to grow
Now gone blank hearted
            My sanity has departed . . .

Gigantic daydreams play out
            Into my soul without a doubt
Taking me away to that better place
            I disappear without a trace . . .

            Never to be found again;
Today, the Angels finally win.

MY FRIENDLY PAIN

I can close my eyes & see You
Feeling your hair tickle my Face
As we embrace, your kiss to Trace . . .

The sweet air that surrounds You, There
I take a deep breath, to breathe You
Straight into me, so Free . . .

Holding still, standing in that place with You
Not ever wanting anything else, Ever
Becoming part of what is truly New . . .

Every time this happens we are together, Again
I feel these things all over, the Same
But just a bit more than Before . . .

It is my friendly pain that enters Me
When ever You must Leave
I can close my eyes & see you.

AND NOW IT IS TIME TO SAY GOODBYE

Watching her go, I had a thought:
Now, this is the end of the end.
Stable but shaken & a bit distraught;
I realized our marriage we failed to mend . . .

Torn forever,
This time.
Better to sever,
For lack of rhyme . . .

Knowing all along,
This day would come
I tried to stay strong,
At least strong to some . . .

And finally, This:
(In just the blink of an eye)
I blew her a kiss-
And now it is time to say goodbye.

The Great Blank Minutes

As the neon light quietly covers everything in view
Great silence of blank minutes hums straight through
Reality fades to the back ground of a psychedelic scheme
Trapped in the Numb-Dane, hear comes another wide-eyed dream . . .

Falling deep within the electronic data haze
Finding something that was lost had brought on better daze
Avid touch from a long-lost Lover, created within
Remembering our heated lust exchange is where my sin begins . .
.

Manifesting these memories within my embattled attention span
Shows pictures of our innocence, like when we first held hands
These images hold true & pure forever to remind-
Of the past that could not last, nor can we ever rewind . . .

Crashing back into the track that is this lonesome place
I awaken to the sound of the phone ringing in my face
My last thoughtful thought is that you are somewhere fine
And that you have finally found the One for you, Divine.

Care to Have

Thoughts & dreams of deep compassion
Are things of a forever fashion?
Worn by the heart to easily stay warm
In even the coldest emotional ice storm . . .

Please, find inside what was there, all along
Within True Love is where we Belong . . .

To care to have it is so such the need
That without it—Heart cannot be freed
There is nothing left to save-
Looking forward, becoming Brave.

Requiem for a Tear

The heat from my tears
    Reminds me of your sweet embrace.
As they flow down my lonely face,
    A silhouette of your heart they trace . . .

Once,
    Soaked into my skin
The circle begins, again
    &
I remember-
    That not a thing can stop the Sun from
rising
The light of a new day-
    That draws me closer to you is
surely shining . . .

As sure as the world is turning
    My heart is beating
        To Love you, on purpose.

Silent Apologies

If I say "I am sorry", without saying a word
For an unknown wrong of which you have not heard;
Does it heal the invisible bleeding inside,
Or make it complete, opening it up wide?

Until that one day when your heart does not show;
Too heavy from every white lie ever told.
Slowly, but certainly, all is revealed.
Minus silent apologies, forever concealed . . .

They lay, kept away-
In a secret, mythical storage space.
It is right next to the perfect paradise we used to chase.
If I say "I am sorry", without saying a word?

PIECES

Intenseness of overwhelming desire
Runs through my veins;
The bright spark that starts a fire,
Just before it rains . . .

Your Love guarded within my heart
As we wallowed in imperfection;
We were torn apart
We made one wrong
selection . . .

When times are tough, we must be strong
I make your beautiful body shake;
You make myself belong
So much is at stake . . .   Our passion is invincible
The quest is true;
We will pick up the pieces
~Just me & you.

Lonely Man's Want Ad

Ache away, my mysterious desire;

      Seek, until you find & get what you deserve.

Bring it in, to your temple's sire;

      Who would die to give it preserve . . .

I seek, I need, I call to the one,

      This is my formal decree:

Who is to claim this task as done?

         Who is to set me free?

I will not ever turn down this flame-

      The world is to see it's shine!

Into tomorrow without shame;

      Into Destiny, Heaven's own design.

HOME-COOKED CONFUSION

Sugar donuts frolic among star crunching pop-tarts
Dry goods are playing games with each other
The chicken in the freezer counts it's parts
I saw this all & screamed for my mother . . .

Chef Boyardee gets a solid microwave tan
While Betty Crocker hides a bun in the oven
The scoop is that the dough-boy is her man
But, he is busy giving Dolly Madison lovin' . . .

Cigarettes smoke & give themselves cancer
So that Twinkies can live always.
(Long live the Twinkies!)
Macaroni and Cheese is a pretty good dancer
Depending on the gig & how well it pays.

The Edge of Tomorrow

So, to have any burden released is to drop the point~ Instead of
carrying it to the edge of tomorrow?

A blanket that covers all of your fears, that even
covers the Lowest of a leveled heart—Is always
Just out of reach when your lover is away . . .

These simple facts are known only to the parties
Involved in a Love that will have no End~
No, I do not expect you to understand . . .

Like it, or leave it behind a wall of forgotten yesterdays;
Piling up, faster & faster until, One day-
All you have left are yesterdays . . .

To rummage through stacks & rows of memories in your
Mind's time. Is this why we exist? To create
A huge spirit-base filled with all emotional information~
For our creator to collect on judgment day?
Will ~HE~ add them to a collection of beautiful~
Conscious realities built from all Humanity?
What is not to Love?

Red Love Journal Entry #1

~I ache to feel Red Love inside of the cavernous valleys
　　　　　　Throughout my heart, Once Again!
~Wait of the world on my shoulders
　　　　　　Could cause a little dismay, nor delay.
~My walk is a swift growth
　　　　　　Toward a true and deliberate salvation . . .

~My articulate coincidence has an unseen chance
　　　　　　Of having reason.
I continue forward into future sunsets . . .
(I can hardly wait)!

Suede

Troubling dreams:

A ruby red crescendo crosses brutal feathers
Softly bruising Love's laughter
    Velvety vengeance melted, delicious;
        Your taste so sweet & warm . . .

        Alluring beauty, glistening in the air,
    delicate & rare;
    A silky soul with a romantic role
        (Is my mysterious Muse with an unseen use)?
        A beauty inspired prize, very small in size:

These troubling dreams:
        Who knows what it means?

Kiss & Tell

Slippery numbness clicks,
Onto cluttered hands it sticks
All the while time passes by
Following feelings of wondering—why?

Plans to kiss you are already there
Letting lips connect is only fair
Remember what you learned so well,
Never, Ever Kiss & Tell.

Substance

**Mystical motion of radiance
Spills out of gigantic hand-held creation . . .**

**Nourishment of Omnipotence begins to dance
Causing power spindling vibration . . .**

**Constellating systems combine thrust & rhythm
Protecting purpose filled coincidence . . .**

**Driving explosions climax to a rumbling hum
Conceiving the spiritual experience.**

STAGE RIGHT ANSWER

Setting the stage is a trained sixth sense
Directing my rage against stormy future events
> Honesty conducts wind to play the symphony of truth~
>> While deception blows thin my supply of youth . . .

Hesitation could not wait to lose it's chance
Leading my desire to a five star performance
> Seductifying options dance to decision~
>> As consequence concludes climax with skillful precision . . .

Critics of all hindsight look back in full view
Pondering the differences in what they would choose
> Destiny commanding fate is always the same~
>> No matter what play you are in, or how you spell your ~NAME.

The Light at the End

I found myself at an all-time low
Due to falling down a solar-sized hole
Ready to give up and in, all within
The light at the end was your lovely grin . . .

The deep darkness had captured me, falling
Until your beauty, alive—I felt it's calling
Cold hands had held everything tossed,
When your Love came abound to reclaim the lost . . .

Taken & kept for good, forever
Protected by all that is clear and clever
Our passion has been tested, tried & true
Fueled by what this Love holds for Me & for you.

STILL

It is my choice to Love You
Have this Love for You, I will
Part of the luckiest few
As long as my heart beats still . . .

There can be no missed solace
In the tight depth of your embrace,
In the tenderness of your Kiss,
Or in the light of your pretty face.

Stand by Me

If I had a dollar

For every time I cried

There would be a river of money

Mountains deep, Oceans wide . . .

If I could spend it all,

Finally setting my soul free

I would choose to be broke

If only standing alone with thee.

On the Tips of our Wings

Arabian nights have only dreamed of days
  That I will have Loved You in so many ways . . .

To see the golden glow
  That I have longed to know~
    Skin changes colors,
      In preparation to be uncovered . . .

Reaching that awesome moment in which we achieve
  The pinnacle of affections each to receive . . .

Through endurance of inept seclusion:
  Thoughts of You are much of my delusion . . .
Wings of night fly on cosmic flights
  & touch our air with these romantic delights.

IN THE AIR, AS YOU WERE WALKING BY

Eloquently exiting fragrances fill~
The displacement of your surrounding air;
These full flavors swim by my will~
Dancing in the heart of chaos with care . . .

Memories made of this momentary space~
Become a spice within the perfect sort;
Entwined with a ribbon of Angel's lace~
And invisible flights of passion, too short.

My Wild, Wreck less Abandon

We should kiss like we kissed
    On the day that we did
        In the way we were kids . . .

We could have cared less
    We could not have shared more;
Our bodies do confess~
    (This wild wreck less Abandon, Do explore!)

Our hearts will find Love's Design
    To give each kiss a polished shine.
        These lips that touch do belong
            In that place which is never wrong.

THE PERFECT SLOW DANCE

I could sustain my life by making your pleasure
The flowing fountain from which I feed
All the little things you do are my treasure
In the Paradise of Growing Need . . .

Sunshine seduces the grace of your skin
As Desire fulfills Destiny, yet again
Waves of passion washing through the tides of Time
Give way to our heat, knowing only how to rhyme . . .

Never let the night fall upon the steps of this chance
Hold the Moon away from any luminous advance
To sail beyond the sunset into this endless Romance
We must teach our deepest dreams
The most Perfect Slow Dance.

Happiness Is . . .

Hands on hold of my soul's control,
Satisfying the need to know,
&
Knowing your part in God's grand show.

Happiness Is . . .

Pleasure filled bliss
Never to miss
Touch with your kiss.

Happiness Is . . .

Felicity making anew
Daydreams that do come true
&
Finally, Irrevocably
"I Love" rhyming with "You".

Sunshine's Design

When looking into your eyes, without compromise
The bluest skies are never a surprise
These emotions are in motion, so intense-
Propelled by our feelings of dense suspense . . .

Life is growing, Love is promoting
These two smiles, gently floating
Planned out with very intricate design
Combined with Sunshine we consign to the Divine.

Hear & Now

There it was, right ahead of us,
In the view of all the new between us:
Tiny little things sparkle -&- glisten
As the light passes through
Small beads of priceless sweat . . .
As if in the desert, and this is our rain . . .

There is no pain, just an ache~
Welcome as it draws us to one another
With unseen Force; As if we share
A supernatural magnetic-field of Dreams . . .

Sew it seems, clear as the sky in your eyes
~The Future~
Bright as the light that barely glides between
Our softness, Leaving a shadow on our past . . .
We are together, At last!

Turn of the Tide

My hands slide across, sooo smooth
    The curves of your sexy body sooth;
        The peach tint satisfies my craving
            We savor the flavor, misbehaving . . .
                Fitting together, oh, sooo well
                We could not be farther from any Hell
            The perfect paradise is taken by this demand
    In the middle of you, I find the Promised Land . . .
There is no shame in letting down our guard
    The opposite of me, It couldn't be less hard
        You slowly search over every inch of me
            To finally find the truth:
                To be or not to be free?
                This intense overwhelming flood of fire
            Punctuated by Nirvana built to inspire
    Suddenly concludes, needing to subside
Until the next wonderful Turn of our Tide.

Love Potion Commotion

Dangerous Destiny
    Awaits downright despair˜
      As my delicious desire
                H
                  A
                    N
                      G
                        S˜
              __Brilliant in air;__

    A massive combination of Emotional Commotion,
(Along with romantic sparks mixed in my secret Love Potion)˜
Freeze the moment with a culmination of Angel's spice
    Acrimony drowns in the color of Love, All things Nice . . .

    The final result is a True Love story:
      Lived through elegance of Grace˜
        The favor of Glory.

Handful of Whispers

Gazing upon opportunistic sunsets of the heart
I realize this nurtured touch from the start
Eager selves magnetized by the desire within
Looking ever so forward to holding one another, again . . .

A handful of whispers are remembered & kept
Waiting for anxious eyes prepared to accept
Faithfully thought out plans & dreams
Take such careful time sewing seems . . .

Wanting becomes needing/A thin line to separate:
Two different romances with the same noble fate
Concentrated souls, lonely no longer
With every passing kiss the fire is stronger.

The Darkness Slayer

Standing totally alone, upon the horizon I see
Every monstrous demon coming to devour me
Wandering not, these creatures come with fierce purpose
Becoming clear, I realize their vast surplus ...

Shuddering within myself, I know I have created each one
I am my own worst enemy and now my soul is coming undone
Anger, Hate, Greed & Lust lead an army against my will
In that moment, thinking all was lost ~HE~ made them be still ...

Frozen within his presence, their advance made futile
Just then, ~HE~ took my hand & said, "Walk with me awhile".
Weeping with Awe & regret ~HE~ wiped tears from my eyes
~HE~said "I am here to remind you, my child, my gift is no surprise".

Then, ~HE~ lifted me up above the muted battleground below
Flying across the sky with 10,000 Angels in tow
Taking me home to where I belong
Never to forget: They are weak, but ~HE~ is Strong.

Fist full of Faith

Holy things never have shadows,
~For they are a part of light~

Bask within their rays, eyes closed,
~Beginning flight~

Straight Love

You are the Light, You are the way—
Giving true sight, as I pray . . .

Lift me up & sink me in—
After all, you still vanquished our sin.

You are all that we will ever need—
Within your Love our dreams are freed . . .

Faith & Hope follow Love, so well—
When in our hearts, Anyone can tell.

Thank you, Lord—Forgiving us all—
Only through this Love can we hear you call . . .

Its not too late to set this world straight—
Let us do away with hate
To open Heaven's Gates.

The Amazing:

1) The way humans treat each other.

2) Both of my sisters, along with my brother.

3) A kiss, a hug, or a single drop of hope.

4) The true size of a nuclear isotope.

5) Caring acts of random Kindness.

6) Our humanity and the ties that bind us.

7) The simple nature of a romantic encounter.

8) My true Love & the day I find Her.

9) The Holy Bible & all of God's Glory.

10) Romeo & Juliet's True Love story.

STIMULUS

As the corners of your mouth
    E to the occasion of the brightest smile
    S
    I   There is a tiny tweak in your cheek . . .
R

I know the source of this expression
    Starts in the fire ignited by You & I,
The strongest of desires-
    The shine in your eye . . .

Hungry for the heat that only comes through us
    To hold anything back would be so unjust
Finally letting go of all reserve
    Giving to each other everything we deserve.

Paradise Tasted

True partners-in-crime
Let's take the honey and run!
Making Love rhyme all the time . . .

Coupled together with a tantric hypnotic blaze
Tested in this fire, we certainly have been
So deserving of our wonderfully chaotic daze . . .

Never having a moment wasted
While sharing our wasted moments
A kiss from you is paradise tasted.

Touch you More

Let me open your doors

     & cook you smores;

Work hard to lay your floors

     & do your chores

I want to be there to cover you

     When it pours

I cannot wait to touch you more . . .

     Your beautiful everything not to be ignored~

As there lies paradise galore with forever

     To explore

       You rock me through to my very core~

As it has never, ever been done before.

THIS TIME

Seeming fragile, the seconds slip away pure
Another exercise of patience that we must endure
Moment by moment as this time marches on
Our Love stands still, intolerance be gone . . .

Loving you is my most simple of task
To have my all, you must not even ask
However imperfect my mind, my heart beats so true
When you are away it fades to a very deep blue . . .

Aching, burning torment is worth every single sting
For even a moment of the passionate Love that you bring . . .
The wanting and needing is my subliminal sign~
Of what your touch does to me, while you are mine.

Two Become Won

Deep, Once boundless Lovers
    Become irrevocably delicious
Leaving inelegance to further solitude . . .

Phantom versus desire, two worlds collide
    (Stealing the ability to exist at all)
Against the real, imagined distinction between
hearts . . .

A new dimension created, only they could share
    (Once alone, Two become Won)
Laugh indelibly, walking on the Sun.

Stealing these Moments

There is a swelling in my body, so sublime

Connecting with you makes it all rhyme

The moments spent memorizing your delicate face

Bend reality to form our own time & space . . .

Fulfilling each other's wanted need of Love driven thirst

Drinking you, swallowing me, we know what comes first

The touch of our bodies together in masked paradise

Finding Arcadia within our reach, the only price . . .

Feeling slow luminosity burning within our

                         Passion's Core

Unable to resist it, our clothes end up on the floor

Naked motion spills out of this dream come true

Stealing these moments, Life spent with You.

Love Note

My lover, I long to learn new words to tell~
Of all the ways of "In-Love" I fell
With You, the view is truly anew
As clear as the diamond we see forever through
Within our deepest embrace,
The dreams are warm and commonplace~
I MUST Kiss your dreamy face, Over & Over and
Over again ...

**Somehow, Now,
Someway, Today~**
I write these words to make them say:
I love you, I love you, I love you!!!

KNOWING

Letting that emotion win, Again & Again
Now & Then, we still take it in the chin,
Defending until the End . . .

This, too, we will mend
All I have is Love to send
I will never, ever pretend . . .

KNOWING THIS KNOWS THAT SHOWING THIS GROWS
THE HEART THAT STANDS TALL AGAINST LOVE'S FOES.

More than Anything

All of our energies splashed into this task
Is a dream come true really too much to ask?
We will answer this question for ourselves to be sure
That the final result is a product of Love, so pure . . .

Never giving up, Never letting go
Never say never is for someone else to know
This fight is for our right to exist in our ways
& have so many more passion filled romantic days . . .

When it all seems to much to go on & sustain
The glow of our fire will always remain
Giving us the reason to continue for tomorrow
Vanquishing all the defeat & memories of sorrow.

Speechless

The search is done
Our two became One
Enchanting times we share
Yes, Love is in the Air . . .

Simple & True
"I Love" rhymes "with You"
As easy as this:
Remember that first Kiss?

In many moments & In many ways
With You I will share the rest of my Days
Sparkly glitter all around our space
I Love to Kiss your beautiful Face . . .

Not to mention the rest of your shape
I do find this a great escape~
No other option could capture me speechless
That is, Unless . . .

☺ Smile ☺

When you smile
    My whole world gets three shades brighter.
Then, You giggle & laugh-
            Making the space between us
                    Mysteriously tighter . . .

The way the tip of your nose
    Tweaks when you grin;
            Moves me to make it happen, again & again . . .

You make me so happy, too!
    Smile again, so that I can smile with you. ☺

SHADOWS

Hidden in the shadows of the pillars
That hold Heaven in the sky, so High;
True Love awaits both You & I . . .

Satin glances of innocent purities pour
Through my heart, leaving me wanting
More . . .

Touch is the gateway to the Kingdom
of my Caress . . .
These feelings for you, I must Confess.

The Shape of things to Come

There have been so many empty days
Hollow moments, lost in a maze:
~Without You~

The time has been stretched out, so long
My soul constantly searching to belong:
~There is no other place~

Our shiny minutes can be seen all, everywhere
When you are near me with nothing left to bare:
~My Love Can Survive~

Now, it is my turn to tell you what I know
To let my actions & my words truly show:
~I am in Love with You~

~Without You~
~There is no other place~
~My Love Can Survive~
~I am in Love with You~

Scrumptious Clichés

Captured on that photogenic trap
Never to fade like youthful age
Still frames in time, space & gap
Carry over uneventful rage . . .

Scrumptious clichés of happy sex
Heating up the light of the Sun
Where in Love- What comes next-
Getting bright, second to None . . .   Tickling every section of your spot
Rolling over, Never get caught
Holding me down, Again! Again!
You feel so good, this must be a Sin . . .

Then in the end & I do not mean last-
Why must these moments fly past, so fast?
Your sweetness of skin, I must confess,
Have my thoughts all
~Undressed.

HEAVEN HOLDS TIGHT

Let our lifelong journey through Love shine through
As the stars in the sky are for me, for you

Come into my realm of decorated memories
Stay for a moment; Forever if you please

Concentrated drops of desire rain around & near
Our place inside to wash away, making clear

There is something special in effortless tries
Like the noises heard in devotional sighs

Holding each other, Heaven holds tight
Love's sincere breath tonight

True Illusions

Making sense has gone away & far
Who cares? As long as we ARE . . .

Making our Love the best we know how
No body can say that our time is not Now . . .

Hold your head high, chin stout, Smile.
"I think I will Love you for awhile", she said
Whispering thoughtfulness of Dreams~
Into my soul, with locked-in moon beams . . .

Portraits of our happiness drawn on a sidewalk with chalk
Everyday, hand in hand, together we walk
Follow me into fantasy filled futures of tomorrow
Never letting go of what it means to feel sorrow . . .

Protecting my heart from breaking in two
Your Love, the only illusion that is true.

HOLD YOUR EYES & CLOSE YOUR BREATH

Open my eyes to the peach of your skin
Stretching my body hard & Then
Rubbing my eyes puffy & thick
Grabbing You is such a happy trick!

Smiles contain my crowded heart
A kiss on the lips is where to start
Anxious to feel your bright embrace
I never want to leave this place!

All is clear, this adoring moment
Aching for you is focused torment
Sliding over, touching me, indeed
Finally, You show the need:
F
    A
       L
         L
Into place, you know the rest . . .
Just close your eyes and Hold your breath.

LOST & FOUND

My lips find the soft part of your peachy cheek
The desire to leave them there makes me weak
My mind fills with smoldering hot thoughts, eyes closed
My heart races lightning fast; In your arms it knows…

As our bodies connect in rhythm & rhyme
These awesome moments seem to stop all time
Neither one of us knowing how or why
It flies by in just the blink of an eye…

Knowing that we will always be wanting more
Of knowing each other so well, to the core
This passion filled devotion, truly kind
Within each other it is ourselves we find.

SIMPLE

You completely fulfill my thoughts & dreams
All while defining our life's wonderful themes
Without your Love I was so lost & cold
Now, I excitedly wait for each day to unfold . . .

I still cannot believe that you actually chose me
An honor it was, to get down on one knee
Every day spent that includes you in my life
Amazes me anew knowing that you are my wife . . .

So many things readily shared
Time played out alone does not compare
When you read these lines, feel the passion, too
It is as simple as I SO Love You!!!

And then there was You

To not ever give up for what you need-
Knowing one day that heart will be freed . . .
Send the message to all concerned-
Defeat takes much more than getting burned . . .

Now, I can see beyond the trees,
Through the forest, beyond raging seas . . .
Tiny moments unraveling in time-
Sharing all of it with my someone, in rhyme . . .

Someone to touch this life that is shared,
Like new Love & second chances compared . . .
To have, to hold to follow all the way through-
I looked up, And then there was You.

Plus One

Hundreds of verses written just for you
    A map of my heart to give you a clue
If even one direction should be Untrue ~
    I will burn them all & start anew . . .

So, here is another to brighten your day;
    Add a page to this book, now on display
All the Love found as we have grown
    Teaches us soft what once was unknown . . .

Stronger still we are today than before
    My heart stands at your call wanting more
Give me simple affections authored & owned
    One plus One equals never alone.

Closure . . .

The true feelings of Love, heated
A smile, a laugh, to feel again
Heartache of a memory defeated
. . . I stand, wiping tears from my chin

Thoughts of what we had, fade
Hope is in a hug, hidden
Remembering the romance made
. . . You leave, your happiness forbidden

Giving fear strength in the moment ahead
An idea—Your sadness, to let it go
Disabled dreams shattered, now dead
. . . You have always been your own worst foe

Closure comes as a matter of fact
The sacred hearts' fire was & IS right
I will wake up tomorrow, desire intact
. . . New energy born, the compassion to fight

A very special '*Thank You*' goes to:

GOD,

(ALL OF MY FAMILY~ INCLUDING BUT NOT LIMITED TOO:
AMY BETH & OUR 3, MOM & MY LATE DAD, GENA & HER 3,
CANDY & RAY & 3 R'S, PAPA JOE, BILL GATHINGS (SR. & JR.),
RYAN & JAIME MCLEMORE, TASHA,
THOMAS MAGDELANO,
STORMIE SCHUBERT,
DANNY WINTERS,
DOUG & TAMI,
SUE HUGGINS,
NATALIE MULLINS,
LORI GOREE & HER FAMILY,
E.E. CUMMINGS, MARK TWAIN,
ROLO TOMASI, KEISER SOSAI,
ROBERT A. HEINLEIN, E. & B.,
MY BRO~JIM EVERETT (COVER-ARTIST & GENA LOVER),
EFG COMPANIES & EVERYONE THERE WHO GAVE/GIVES SUPPORT,
ANYONE WHO EVER HAS OR WILL CALL ME 'CRAZY',
'FUNNY', DORKY, OR 'WEIRD'.
ALL OF MY MUSICAL INSPIRATIONS~
(ESPECIALLY: S.T.P. & THE CURE.)
LAST BUT DEFINITELY NOT LEAST:
MY ALWAYS LOVE, SWEETS &
ALL OTHERS THAT HAVE EVER
BROKEN MY HEART
(YOUKNOWWHOYOUARE)

WHAT DID YOU DO WITH YOUR PAIN?

~KEEP DREAMING~
(UNTIL YOUR DREAMS COME TRUE.)

Edwards Brothers,Inc!
Thorofare, NJ 08086
13 April, 2011
BA2011103